Sex Gam
for Couples

*Play Naughty and Fun Sex Games to
Rekindle the Spark in Your
Relationship and Awaken Sexiness,
Seduction, and Ecstasy
(2022 Guide for Beginners)*

Eloise Hardy

TABLE OF CONTENTS

INTRODUCTION

Intercourse is a sexual act that expresses your passion, excitement, caring, and other strong feelings for another person. It is an enthralling and intense event that may bring two people even closer together. Lovemaking should be a time when you and your spouse feel free, comfortable, and optimistic. Regardless of whether this is right, many people are concerned when the thought of having intercourse comes to mind because they are attempting to figure out what the proper way to have intercourse is.

A large percentage of women are unable to realize their enjoyment potential because their partner has a limited understanding of what lovemaking is. (Whether you are straight, gay, single, married, weird, poly, trans... it doesn't matter... you may change this lovemaking approach to suit your sexual delight.)

Sex extends beyond the first stage of invasion. All of your actions are not laying the road for intercourse. When you understand how to get a woman into her sexual personality condition and then provide her stacking, increasing orgasmic delight, the whole lovemaking backdrop may be euphoric. You must connect with yourself before making the step to have intercourse. What is the current state of your regard? Confidence has a significant impact on your lovemaking displays. If there is anything specific about yourself that makes you nervous, make it your goal to overcome that uncertainty. Continue to chip away at it until you reach a level of security that you are happy with.

Great and spectacular lovemaking does not happen in a secret way that is unrelated to everyone else. It requires effort and study. If you and your partner have agreed to be intimate and are experiencing sexual movement together, there is no need for you to be afraid of probing one other's body. Take as much time as you need to appreciate and connect with your partner's body's intricacies. Genital touch has a higher impact than the overwhelming majority of people believe. Observing your partner's physique can increase your gratitude for that individual while also stimulating you. The individual will also feel happy and unusual, which is always a good thing!

Discussing your intimacy with your companion may make you feel embarrassed or foolish, but it is something to consider if you are not obtaining what you want and require behind those room entryways. If you don't talk about it, your discontent will grow until you no longer want to have sexual relations with your spouse. You two are comfortable enough with one other to see each other naked, so talking about it shouldn't be a problem. Regardless of whether you are generally content with your lovemaking schedules, chatting despite everything is beneficial to your relationship since you will acknowledge each other's exceptional lovemaking abilities, cherish one another, and bring you closer together.

Exercise regularly needs a good warm-up to show indicators of better outcomes. The same is true for having intercourse.

You should never rush into it since it displays how little value you have on the close time you enjoy with your spouse. Of course, there will be instances when you need to be unrestrained and just lay it all on the line, but at the end of the day, you can't simply request it and accept it. Add some emotional touches to your lovemaking strategy. Models include going out to your favorite nostalgic café, watching the sunset on the beach, watching a movie you both like, giving each other an erotic massage, scrubbing down together, and so on. Find out what works best for you!

Couples who have been together for a long period will never desire to play with each other again. They believe that is something people do when they are single and trying to score with someone. Being a tease is a lot more fun when you're seeing someone. You both know each other and have a feeling of safety, which makes you more willing to express whatever is on your mind. So, go ahead and play with your companion and irritate that individual who has entered the room!

CHAPTER 1:

HOW TO IMPLEMENT COUPLE GAMES IN YOUR BEDROOM

Long-term partnerships and living in the same place introduce a plethora of daily habits into our life; obstacles begin to destroy desire, and sex quickly becomes the same "Saturday habit." This occurs regularly because everyday concerns and life issues take precedence over romantic nights together, as they do in the first few months of a candy bouquet relationship.

Unspoken dissatisfaction, unsolved difficulties, or accumulated aggressiveness should not exist in your family life, since they lead to quarrels, resentment, and a chilly and uninteresting bed. Sexual games are a means to relieve everyday tension, have fun, promote sensuality and sexuality, and not upset each other, but rather ignite. In-bed role-playing games allow you to turn into a character and behave in ways you would never dare to do in real life. This change allows you to be less shy, to choose your words and actions more carefully, since you both realize that this is only a game.

Some family conflicts may be solved by role-playing in bed. How does it function? The game's roles might be highly diverse, but the story is much more significant. For example, in every partnership, one partner always has the upper hand. In the role-playing game, you may swap roles: if the spouse makes choices in normal life, you can become a harsh teacher and punish him for his poor conduct. Also, a typical issue in relationships occurs when we direct our collected anger and unhappiness onto a partner, although a loved one is not to blame for your shortcomings at work or in other areas of life. Transfer difficulties outside the house to the game so that they do not reflect in the relationship. Allow a guy to be the boss that night and write you a few reprimands if he returns home after a heated dispute with his employer.

Script, Rules, and Inventory for a Role-Playing Game

First and foremost, consider the obstacles and innuendos in your relationship. If you've never played sexual games before, this strategy will assist you in learning the initial roles and relieving tension in the plane of relationships where it has gathered. Incorrect roles or scripts may devastate a whole production. Consider a guy who is continually upset because his girlfriend has been cursed at him for whatever reason and without, and here he is given to play mistress and her page-boy - the same circumstance that generally occurs. Even if a guy accepts, this game is unlikely to provide him with pleasure, which, as with any sexual encounter, should be reciprocal.

Try to gently guide your spouse to what concerns him, find painful areas, and capture unexpected words, but don't speak about it openly, otherwise, you risk turning everything into a minor household scandal rather than a pleasant game. Then, choose the responsibilities that will allow you or your companion to "recoup." It will not be unnecessary to learn about his fantasies, but everyone has them. Write a short, easy scenario so that the game does not come to a halt or move in the incorrect direction (for example, you should have been mistress, but then the guy took the initiative again). It is not essential to consider all of the talks in minute detail, but the basic direction should be defined.

Sexy outfits are quite important in erotic games.

Another approach for deciding on roles is to go inside yourself: consider what you want to explore, what sensual ideas visit you, and what sort of attire or surroundings you want.

The next step is to outfit. It's a lot of fun to dress up. And knowing what kinds of garments might excite your sexual urge can make this activity much more pleasurable and interesting. Sexual vibration may be found in even the most mundane of items. Everything is easy here - either go through your wardrobe for appropriate clothing (for example, you will almost certainly find something for the job of a teacher or boss) or visit a sex store (not every home has a nurse's robe or a pilot's outfit). When you've decided on the costumes, consider what equipment could be required so that you don't have to dash about the apartment amid the game looking for a pointer, stethoscope, or pipi aster - everything should be nearby.

Role-Playing Requirements

The game starts a couple of hours before the auction begins. Send a themed message to your spouse (for example, "Doctor, I have a headache; may I see you tonight?"). - Since you're already playing, ignore the mundane prompts like "Buy bread." Similarly, you may leave a hidden letter for your spouse, but you must ensure that he finds it. It'd be a pity if you placed it in your trouser pocket and he wore jeans.

Do not begin if you are unsure that you will finish. The worst thing you can do is tease each other with texts throughout the day and then change your mind at the last minute. Such detours will not help your relationship.

Do not change your clothing or get ready in front of each other. You must meet for the first time in full uniform and clothing, otherwise, the "magic" will not function.

Continue playing to the finish. None of the partners amid the game can remove their suits and exit the game. To begin with, sex faces the danger of passing as normal and failing to perform the psychological function for which it was initiated. Second, you risk offending a partner's efforts, exacerbating the relationship's troubles.

Improvise. Do not panic if the game slows down because you did not have a ready-made script or it was not integrated. The words "I'm not sure what's next," "Think about it yourself," and "Maybe you can play along with me?" are forbidden! It's best to plan ahead of time where the story could go and what to do if it does. In any case, even if you discover a problem with interpersonal communication during the game, do not focus on it; instead, turn your attention to any aspects that pleasantly excite you in this situation, shift the focus to the exciting details, to immerse yourself in the game deeper and avoid losing your sexual mood. After that, you may ponder and calmly address any areas for development in a more appropriate setting.

Avoid attempting to be a superb actor. It is unnecessary to read Hamlet's monologues in front of the companion. Concentrate on the primary aim of the game: excellent sex. If you're not playing as George Clooney, trust me, your spouse is unlikely to notice and will almost surely not criticize you.

Do not exaggerate the importance of others' roles. Do not drag the blanket over yourself if your spouse is the dominant figure in the circumstance. Similarly, if you dominate, don't allow the partner to get the better of you; you'll have to be harder, but not too difficult; for rookie players, the line is fairly thin. It is advisable to explain the guidelines ahead of time.

Do not undress beforehand. If you took off you're clothing on each other right away, the game has already failed since the highly intriguing stage of flirting has been gone.

It may seem trite, but certain sexual games, particularly those involving BDSM devices, need the usage of "stop" phrases. The term should be simple yet out of character for the narrative. If you are playing in a clinic, for example, you should not select a "dropper" with a stop word; instead, consider something unusual, such as a "bullfighter" - it is doubtful that you would discuss the bullfight in the script.

You should be home alone at this time; the phones should be turned off.

You should be as delicate as possible; sometimes even a harmless joke may ruin the atmosphere, and the spouse will reject similar entertainments in the future.

Don't think about anything else; if in the height of the game, a kitten suddenly declares, instead of "murmur," that she has to contact her mother tomorrow, this drastically disrupts the atmosphere.

CHAPTER 2:

SEX ROLEPLAYING GAMES

Role-playing is a simple and enjoyable approach to overcome sexual inhibitions. Sexual role play is a game that includes playing out sexual fantasies using various roles that may be entirely different from the people in real life. The intensity of the game is determined by the players. You may opt to role-play with improvised props or go all out with scripts and matching costumes for each part of the show. To enjoy sexual role play, you do not need to be an award-winning actor/actress or even have any previous acting experience.

The Procedure
Bring Up Your Mutual Sexual Aspirations

Unless you want to catch your spouse off guard and hope they play along, it is typically best to explore several concepts and situations with your partner. Come up with a solution that both of you believe is acceptable. We all have sexual fantasies, even if we don't want them to come true. However, these fantasies may serve as a guide for you while you engage in role-playing with your spouse. Perhaps you wish your masseur or therapist would be a little braver and push things a little farther during your massage sessions, or you have always had a crush on one of your college professors. Share your dreams with your spouse and discover which ones you can both play out.

This is critical since one partner's concept of role-playing may be too powerful or kinky for the other. But, if you speak it out together, you'll find out what works best for both of you. In any case, it's a good idea to have an open mind and consider it all to be pure imagination.

At first, you may start with minimal settings. Too much detail and creativity may be too much for you or your partner, defeating the purpose of sexual role play. Begin with something that you can accomplish in a comfortable environment, such as your own house or a local restaurant or pub. Choose basic roles/characters and circumstances like:

- A lonely businessman and a soothing attractive lady in a pub or restaurant.
- A perverse instructor and a mischievous pupil in a class or the teacher's office.
- In a hospital bed, a nurse and her ailing patient.
- In the living room or kitchen, a homeowner and his gorgeous maid.

If You Want to Act the Part, Dress the Part

Dress up for the role if it would help you play it more authentically. Hats, wigs, and other costumes may be purchased at costume stores, online, or in adult stores. While costumes may add excitement and fun to the role-playing experience, they are not required. Only purchase them if you believe you really need them.

Furthermore, you may not have additional funds to spend on costumes and props, or you may just choose to keep things simple. Several roles (a stranger at the bar, going on a blind date, and so on) need little to no costume.

Make It Squirmy If You So Desire

Some sexual role-playing situations (for example, cop and criminal, teacher and student, boss and secretary) are more about power and domination.

One partner (the dominant) has complete control over the other (the submit). If you wish to experiment with sexual dominance or kinkiness in a more casual and fun setting, perform the dominant/submissive roles with any character you like.

However, role-playing isn't only about exchanging power. You have the option of avoiding any roles that tend to reflect dominant/submissive characteristics.

Begin slowly.

As is typically the case, it is preferable to take modest steps while embarking on a new endeavor. It may seem too surreal, ludicrous, or just plain dumb to dress up and pretend to be someone else. However, you are not required to dress up in the first place.

Playing pretend may seem to be a juvenile activity, but if you let go and play along for a short time, you may realize that the prospect of picking up a stranger at a bar, for example, turns you on (even if you've known this "stranger" your whole life).

Even if you completely agree with the concept of sexual role play, it is best to begin gently. You might start by sending your lover a dirty text or sext explaining your sexual fantasies. This might be another kind of foreplay. If you are shy, you may utilize this medium to initiate the conversation on potentially unpleasant or humiliating sexual topics.

Allow your character to use foul language.

There is no film director here; just you and your lover. That's why you shouldn't be concerned if you get your first few sentences utterly incorrect. If you fumble or make errors, don't be afraid to joke about it. Nobody is keeping score. Allow yourself to relax into character, and the words will come freely. You may or may not be able to predict how the daydream will conclude. In any case, just allow your imagination to lead you to what your character will say, and then express it without hesitation. Even if you dislike vulgarity or dirty language, your character may. Allow your character to speak anything they need to say to keep the game interesting and thrilling.

Ideas for Sexual Roleplay

Here are a few sexual roleplaying ideas to help spark your imagination and get you started. You are free to modify them to your liking and write your own nasty conversations to go with them. You may use the nasty terms in parentheses in your sex talk.

Pretend you're a fireman who has just saved your spouse and is being rewarded with sex. (It's a dirty phrase: "You saved my life.") The very least I can give you is my dick/pussy.")

. Take on the character of a policeman. Your companion is attempting to wiggle their way out of a speeding penalty. (Another dirty phrase: "The only way out of this is to satisfy me.")

Take on the character of a prostitute who is just interested in having sex for money.

(Dirty phrase: "Show me the money, and I'll give you a nice pussy/cock.")

Pretend you arrived at your friend's house for a sleepover and slipped out to have sex with your friend's sibling. (Dirty phrase: "Shhh... come get a taste of this cock/pussy before anybody notices.")

Pretend you are a customer receiving a massage from your spouse, who is a masseur or masseuse and is eager to provide you with a happy ending. (Dirty phrase: "Could you go a little lower... lower still, sure... that's the place.")

Act as though you knocked on the incorrect hotel room door, but the stranger who opened it (your spouse) let you in nonetheless. (Dirty phrase: "Never mind, I could use someone as beautiful as you right now.")

Assume the position of a landlord who has come to collect their rent, but your spouse is unable to pay, therefore they must pay in kind. (Dirty phrase: "I'm going to fuck my money out of you tonight.")

Pretend you're a yoga teacher, instructing your companion on how to stretch and bend over. (Dirty phrase: "Nice and slow... that's all there is to it. Bring that gorgeous ass over here.")

Assume the position of a supervisor who is ready to have sex with one of his or her employees at the office. (Dirty phrase: "I see you've been stripping me nude all day with your gaze. It's time to transform this work into a sex heaven!")

In a harsh sex session, both of you should play the role of furious partners.

Act as a tour guide with a thick accent. Allow your spouse to hear your naughty conversation in a new accent.

Act out your favorite porn actors' parts from a porn scene or book.

Act as a wicked maid attempting to have sex with the homeowner before the wife arrives. (Cruel phrase: "I'll be in the kitchen...") I'm not wearing any pants. Hurry!")

Pretend to be a dancing instructor and use your emotions to entice your pupil (partner). (Dirty phrase: "Place one foot in front of the other and move your hips in this direction. Gosh! In that stance, you look incredibly attractive!")

Take on the character of a hooker looking for a one-night stand. (Dirty phrase: "I'm free all night.") Do you want to do something hot and fun?")

Take on the character of a pizza delivery man who accepts a blow job in exchange for money. (Dirty phrase: "I'm sorry, but I don't have any money at home. But I'm sure we can come up with a more fascinating method to pay?")

On your wedding night, pretend it's your first sex as husband and wife. (Dirty phrase: "I've been waiting my whole life for this moment. I'm so excited to finally be within you / have you inside me!")

Put on your artist hat and paint your naked lover on a canvas. (Slang: "You have the curves of a god/goddess.")

Pretend you're a bashful virgin having sex for the first time.

(Dirty phrase: "Would you promise to be gentle with me tonight?")

Take on the character of a child who is absolutely clueless about sex. Allow your spouse to teach you how to have sex. (Dirty phrase: "Does it appear like an erect penis/aroused vagina?" Oh... I see.")

Pretend you're a student attempting to charm your instructor in exchange for higher marks. (Dirty phrase: "I may be bad at mathematics, but I can tell by the way you look at me that you want a taste of me, don't you?")

Pretend you are a hypnotist who has successfully mesmerized your spouse. You may order them to do anything you want. (Dirty phrase: "When I teach you, you will suck my cock / devour my pussy.") If you get what I'm saying, nod.")

Pretend you're a nurse and wash your "ill" patient (your spouse). (Dirty phrase: "If you would please step out of your robe, good boy/girl. Now sit back and let me take care of you.")

Pretend to be a striptease and do a lap dance for your companion. (Rough translation: "Do you enjoy it when I bend down and shake my ass like this?")

Pretend you're a taxi driver and have sex with your customer in the rear of your vehicle. (Dirty phrase: "Your objective is still quite a distance away. I propose we take a break here for a little, get a quick food, and have a quickie.")

CHAPTER 3:

TRADITIONAL EROTIC GAMES

In this section, we'll look at some fun games and challenges you may play to spice up your sex life, of the sexy sort, of course. Including erotic games and challenges can make your relationship lively and provocative for a long time, and you can change them up and introduce new ones to keep the experimenting going. In middle school, you might have played innocently flirtatious games like spin the bottle or 7 minutes in heaven.

We're going to employ a familiar concept of fun and games but in a far less innocent form. These games are intended to provide you and your companion with some sexual entertainment. This may be used as foreplay or for fun in the evening. It doesn't have to lead to full-fledged sex, but I guarantee you'll both be so fired up after playing one of them that you won't be able to wait to get to penetration.

Just be careful not to arrive too early in the game.

Never in my life have I

This game is a great way to discover more about your partner's sexual history while simultaneously learning about theirs! You'll both start with your five fingers up, which symbolize your life. One of you goes first and mentions something they've never done before, such as "I've never had a threesome." If your partner has done it, they must raise one finger. You go back and forth like this, and the first player to lose all of their lives is the winner of the game! The loser must then gift the winner anything of their choice. This game may also be played as a drinking game, where instead of using fingers to represent lives, the other person must take a sip of their drink if they have done what you say. Because there are no lives, you can play this way for a long time. To keep it lighter, state things you haven't done that aren't directed at the other person, such as "I've never been called John" if your spouse is named John. Keep it exciting and seductive by mentioning stuff about dating, sex, and any other forbidden themes that come to mind. Play this game to get to know your partner better and for them to get to know you better.

Toss the Bottle

Traditional spin the bottle is done in a big group of people, with each person representing a possible landing spot for the bottle. Everyone forms a circle around the bottle, which is laying on its side in the center. You turn the bottle on its side, and whomever the opening faces when it stops spinning is the person you must kiss.

We're going to shake things up a little with this variation on spin the bottle. You may play this game with anything you have on hand; all you need is a bottle, some paper, and a pen. Consider the traditional spin the bottle circle, in which 6 or 8 individuals sit in a circle. Instead of individuals, we'll have one task at each location. There will be a piece of paper with a challenge written on it at each location, and whichever spot the bottleneck is facing after your spin

Lick my nipples

Give me a hickey

Give me oral sex for 2 minutes

Pick which position we will have sex in after this game

Strip down to your underwear

Give me a message on a body part of my choosing for 2 minutes

Give me a lap dance

I'll hunt for the most bizarre sex position I can find online and you'll try it with me.

Ice/Candle Competition

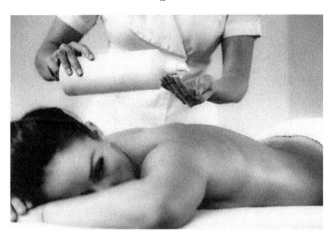

You will need some little ice cubes and a small candle that has been lit for at least a few minutes for this game. To begin, softly massage the piece of ice down your partner's chest between their nipples and down their tummies. This will cause their skin to become chilly and numb. Then, using the candle, gently drip some wax across their chest and down their stomach, in the same locations where you touched the ice cube. Because of the rapid change from cold to heat, their skin will tingle with awareness, and when you touch them, their senses will be heightened. You may even move to other parts of the body, such as the back of the legs or the foot. Have some fun with this as a little foreplay game.

Whipped Cream/Chocolate Competition

The Whipped Cream Challenge is a comparable challenge to the Ice and Candle Challenge. Spread whipped cream or chocolate sauce down your partner's chest to their belly button and down their pelvis, ending just before their sensitive clitoris or the base of their penis. Slowly lick it off of them in the most seductive manner you can think of. You may approach closer and closer to their genitals after you've established the atmosphere for a pleasurable and erotic licking encounter. If you placed chocolate sauce on a man's testicles and slowly licked it off, carefully sucking every last drop off, he'd feel great. He'll go insane seeing you do this. Take turns tackling this task, and then clean up with some warm shower sex.

Dare or Truth

Play a steamy version of Truth or Dare with your spouse. A game of Truth or Dare, much like when you were younger, lets you get to know individuals in a fun and sometimes adventurous manner. If you're unfamiliar with the game, I'll go through the rules first! Each partner alternately asks the other, "Truth or Dare?" The individual answers with their response, and depending on which option they choose, they are given a truth- a question that they must answer truthfully- or a dare- a task that they must perform. They must incur a predetermined penalty if they do not fulfill the dare or refuse to answer the truth question. This penalty may be taking a shot (if you're playing a drinking version) or giving you a massage, or whatever else you like. Decide on this penalty at the start of the game. You will create facts or dares for your companion to tell you or do things to you that are exciting and sexual while you play!

The following are some instances of truths or dares you may tell them:

Truths

Tell me about your craziest sexual dream.

What did you think about/imagine/watch the last time you masturbated.

What is your fondest sexual memory.

What is anything you've always wanted to try during sex.

What is the most heinous thing you've ever done?

Dares:

Lick peanut butter off of any part of your body, ex. finger, chest

Turn off the lights and try to turn the other person on using only sounds

Do a striptease to a song of your choice

Make out with their belly button

Demonstrate their favorite sex position with a pillow

Give them a lap dance

Give them a hickey

Pillow Warfare

What could be better than a good old-fashioned nude pillow fight? Pillow fights are entertaining and flirtatious, and they will take you back to a simpler time. Having a harmless pillow battle with the person you care about can restore a feeling of joy and light-heartedness in your life. This pillow battle will be more fun than any other pillow fight you've ever experienced. When you're both hot and eager from seeing your lover bounce about nude in front of you, go to the bed and enjoy every inch of their gleaming body.

Simon Says Simon Says is another childhood game with a sensual edge. The caller or Simon in this game is one person. This individual may tell the other person to do whatever they want at any time simply stating "Simon says." They may, for example, say, "Simon says, get me a glass of wine." Then, while enjoying their wine, they may remark, "Simon says give me a foot massage."

You may give the individual a time constraint, such as 5 or 10 minutes, to get whatever they want out of it. You may play this game throughout the evening while doing other activities. If you want to concentrate completely on this game, you may take turns saying Simon Says, such that each person gets one turn as Simon, and then it alternates. Begin with simple questions and work your way up to hotter and sexier ones. Make this game as sensual as possible by being imaginative with it.

Game of Sexy Dice

Make a list of 12 sexual actions you wish to conduct with your spouse or acts you want one person to undertake for the other. These might be seductive, adorable, or humorous. Each of them should be written on a separate sheet of paper. Roll two dice together and total the results.

The sex act printed on the paper corresponds to the number you roll. The individual whose number was rolled must then execute the act to or with their partner. Take turns rolling the dice and continuing to do the actions that you are given.

Kiss my feet all over

Suck on both of my nipples for 10 seconds each

Give me a buttocks massage for 2 minutes

Write "I love you" on my tummy with your tongue

Massage a body region of my choice

Give me an orgasm with just your tongue

Tell me your most hidden sexual desire

Trivia About Strips

First, make sure that you and your companion are both wearing the same amount of clothing. Then you'll put your partner's knowledge of you to the test by playing strip trivia! You will each ask the other individual a question about yourself. These questions may be about anything, such as your favorite color, your mother's maiden name, or the house number of your childhood home. If your partner's response is wrong, they must remove one article of clothing. If they get the answer correct, they get to put on a piece of clothes again. If you want to make it more difficult, you may eliminate the second criterion of being able to replace a piece of clothes and determine that if an article of clothing is removed, it is gone for good. You'd best hope you know your spouse better than they know you, or you'll be the first to get nude!

CHAPTER 4

ORAL SEX GAMES

While some may consider oral sex to be a sort of foreplay, I've opted to address it in a separate section for a variety of reasons.

To begin with, there are various misunderstandings regarding it. The first thing to remember about oral sex is that you should be at ease with it, whether you are providing or receiving it. Make certain you're doing it because you want to.

Second, oral sex has the potential to go horribly wrong. There are valid reasons why some individuals refrain from doing so. If you've always thought of oral sex as unpleasant, it's time to alter your thoughts or how you and your partner have been thinking about it.

We will concentrate on how to make oral sex a more rewarding and pleasurable experience for couples.

The Fundamentals of Oral Sex

Before delving further into this topic, let's establish some ground rules. When we engage in oral sex, we often focus on the individual whose genitals are the focus of the activity. However, the one giving the oral does not have to be present only to gratify the other person. The giver should not just lick and drink carelessly. In reality, couples often overlook the fact that when both partners are having fun, the quality of their intercourse improves.

Furthermore, many women often complain about arches, neck pain, or having their mouths dislocated after having oral intercourse. I'm not suggesting that a lot of guys seem to be drilling into the vagina with their fingers instead of appropriately stimulating their partner's erogenous zones. What seems to be common among both guys and females is that they often forget that they can utilize their lips. Oral sex is often conducted only with the tongue.

What you must remember is that oral sex is more than simply "giving." When you shift your viewpoint, you will find that it is no longer tiresome or uncomfortable. When you start thinking about oral sex as a means to fulfill yourself and your spouse, oral sex will become something you both look forward to. In this regard, it is important to dispel certain fellatio fallacies.

First and foremost, a blowjob does not have to be a female-only job. Men should also be willing to engage in oral sex with their partners, and do it enthusiastically and on a frequent basis. The more at ease both parties are with this concept, the more fun it will become over time.

It's obvious that we all appreciate a good blowout now and again. So, the first step is to be willing to contribute without expecting anything in return. Do not wait for your spouse to initiate oral sex. If you're up for it, be the one to propose it to them and see how your spouse responds. Be truthful with your significant other if you want to be the one who receives. While you may feel hesitant about it, being truthful can help you better your sexual and emotional connection.

With this in mind, consider the following before having oral sex with your spouse.

When performing a blowjob, be sure to communicate oneself clearly. We all want to feel like we're doing a good job. This might make us want to keep going; it thrills us and makes us feel attractive. We're in the driver's seat, and we want to know that we're heading in the proper path. If you are getting oral feedback, do not remain mute and compliment your spouse on their excellent effort. Tell your lover how much you're loving every minute of it. On the other hand, if you are the provider, your communication options may seem considerably more convoluted.

However, be creative in expressing to your spouse that you are also enjoying the time. You may groan and make sounds with your tongue, hands, or saliva. Don't assume your spouse is having a good time just because they are the recipient. Instead, pay attention to their movements and gestures. Inform your spouse that you will need his or her assistance if necessary.

It is preferable to have such advice rather than remaining in the same place without your spouse experiencing anything.

Also, keep in mind that comfort comes first. If the recipient is not in a comfortable posture, it will take longer for them to achieve the climax or even have fun. An uncomfortable position, on the other hand, will result in a significantly poorer oral experience.

The recipient or donor may just wish to complete the task as fast as feasible.

If you're going to kneel, be sure to use a comfortable cushion so your legs don't suffer in the end. If you opt to lay on the other person, attempt to find a position in which your knees are not fastened and your neck is not too constricted. Keep your hair pushed back so it doesn't go in your mouth, and shift positions whenever you need to.

Be mindful of your personal hygiene. When it comes to oral sex, nothing is more revolting than untidy genitals.

Furthermore, this is an issue of health precaution. Although you may not have considered it, approaching your partner's genitals immediately after eating some pork ribs is neither clean nor pleasant. Before engaging in oral sex, all you need is a quick wash and a toothbrush. Why not even have some fun in the shower?

Don't forget that you may increase oral sex by using your mouth. When practicing oral sex, keep in mind that your fingers may aid to provide even greater pleasure outside of the mouth. Caress your partner's breasts, thighs, buttocks, or testicles with your hands. Women may stimulate their partners' prostates with their fingertips. Men, too, may use their fingers to treat a portion of the vagina at the same time.

A comprehensive oral sex encounter would be incomplete if you did not use your hands to stimulate the erogenous zones, as previously discussed. Consider this a dual game in which you are double your partner's delight.

Do not disregard the possibility of exciting oneself at the same time. As I previously said, just because you are on the receiving end does not mean you should not enjoy the moment. Masturbate yourself or stimulate your own erogenous zones while doing oral sex with your spouse.

Keep in mind that self-excitement (while performing oral sex) is one of the most critical parts of thoroughly enjoying the act. In addition to merely thinking about it, let your spouse know how much fun you're having. There are several nonverbal methods for doing so, such as glances, gestures, caresses, grins, sighs, and so forth. If you can do this, the experience will be much more pleasurable.

Depilate yourself if it makes things simpler for both of you.

That also applies to guys! Aside from the embarrassment of pulling pubic hair out of your teeth hours after giving a blowjob or cunnilingus, it may be painful for the provider. There is so much pubic hair that you could drown in it! You don't have to remove all of the hair at once; a little trimming may make oral sex much more comfortable for the provider.

Inform your spouse if you are going to ejaculate.

Contrary to what we see in porn, many women do not want to swallow or pour sperm over their faces. To ensure that the grand conclusion is as enjoyable for her as the rest of the encounter, put a hand towards the penis before ejaculating and let her know you are about to finish.

Although female ejaculation is uncommon, many men seem to be unaware when their partners have had an orgasm and will continue conducting oral sex thereafter. It's either because they can't feel the contractions due to the quantity of saliva they're producing, or they're expecting something wonderful to happen. As a result, it is preferable to tell your spouse when you are experiencing an orgasm. It's not only for the purpose of knowing you've arrived at the peak but also so your partner can make the ending even better.

Make certain that your spouse is having a nice time as well. After the climax, do not just go. If you have an orgasm first, make sure your spouse gets a turn as well. Keep in mind that a well-rounded oral sex session should have both participants having a good time.

CHAPTER 5

FANTASTIC EROTIC GAMES

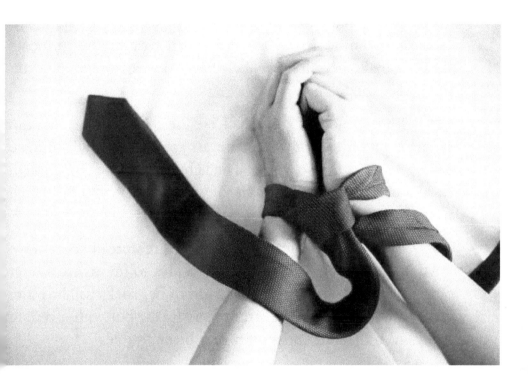

Strip Poker

Strip poker is the most spectacular of the sensual games that may be played in the bedroom. In reality, many people seek for difficult entertainment to arouse desire while the most successful one has been known for decades and can be applied at any moment.

Strip poker, for those who are unaware, is a very basic form of poker in which clothing are used instead of chips. When you "open" your hand or restart your bets, you must state that you are prepared to put your shirt, bra, or underwear on the line. And to give them the thing if you misplace it.

As a result, just a few supplies are required to play with it. Obviously, you'll need poker cards and understanding of the game's rules, but most importantly, you'll need an equivalent amount of outfits. If the lady in the pair wears more garments than the male, he will most likely have to wear something extra to balance the bill.

Furthermore, if you can create the correct mood, this can be a lot of fun. We recommend an appropriate and intimate setting, such as the bedroom. The lighting must be dim enough to allow you to see the fruits of your labor without making everything too noisy.

Finally, if you lose a hand and are forced to remove anything from your body, it is a good idea to improvise a brief strip tease. Of course, seeing the strip of her socks will be more enjoyable than seeing the strip of his socks, but with a certain irony, even the latter possibility may be enjoyable.

Dice Erotica

If you don't enjoy card games, you may skip the fun and go straight to penances. You may get dice that have been expressly manufactured to provide you some unique ideas in specialist and internet shops, for example. There are many sorts and they cost a few euros, but you can also make them yourself if you wish. Simply use regular dice and a conversion chart (1 equates to one punishment, 2 to another, and so forth).

What, on the other hand, may be discovered on the numerous sides of these dice?

For example, in one, there may be activities while in the other, there can be bodily parts. To be more specific, in the first places, such as "kiss", "suck", "pinch", "touch", "blow" or "lick" and in the second areas, such as "chest", "lips", "ears", "neck", "sit", "navel" (or even worse, if you choose).

Other dice, like as Kamasutra, provide advice on sexual positions. They are often dice with 8, 10, or 12 faces with authentic explanatory pictures on all sides. As a result, rolling the dice might compel you to do something you've never done before.

Monogamy

This is the very first true sexy box game ever created. It's called Monogamy, it's made by British Creative Conceptions, and it's widely available in internet retailers. The game provides a gaming board with a circular route for your pawn to follow, and when you wind yourself on different squares, you encounter different cards. These cards, 100 for him and 100 for her, each have three questions with three distinct game levels. There are also 50 fantasy cards included.

The questions, in particular, enable us to analyze the couple's chemistry, and they seem to be spot on for both long-term partners and newcomers. These are inquiries that, in part, probe the other person's thinking, and in part, they propose taking action instead.

Twister Erotica

Monogamy is a game that must be bought and must wait for you to get home. If, however, an erotic game occurs to you at the last minute, when it is already nighttime, you may focus yourself on an alternative option. Change the rules of a traditional box game.

This may be done with any game, and perhaps with particular penances.

Let's imagine you don't have the money to pay when you pass by Victory Park in Monopoly: maybe your spouse can offer you a discount in return for some caresses.

Twister, on the other hand, is a game that, even in its most basic form, is ideal for an amorous evening. Do you recall it? It's the game where you lay a carpet with colored circles on the ground and then turn a little arrow on a dial to figure out where you need to put your hand or foot.

Obviously, when we play in large groups, we end up meeting in odd and inappropriate situations. However, in two stances, they might become slightly seductive. If the standard Twister isn't enough, you may tweak the rules. Perhaps a colored circle should be placed on certain sensitive places of the body ("right hand on green buttock").

Tickling

In reality, in certain parts of the globe, this old ritual has resurfaced with the goal of preparing the pair for sexual intercourse. Tickling, in reality, enables you to generate the appropriate closeness between partners and to touch in areas of the body that are not immediately sexual but are still erogenous.

You do not need to use your fingers, but you may use other tools. A feather, for example, passed on the neck (perhaps behind) or on the back might have a very thrilling impact. Some videos then taught us how to caress our partners using ice cubes, silk ribbons, or even our own hair.

In this scenario, the main thing is to examine the other person's body and determine which spots are the most responsive and sensitive in order to effectively excite them. Furthermore, it would be excellent to postpone the passage "to the facts" as much as possible in order to enjoy this lengthy but lively wait.

Lust

We already mentioned Monogamy, the ideal box game for couples.

Well, it isn't the only one you may utilize to spice up an evening. Another game on the market is Lust, and it's no accident that it's marketed as a "Desire Play," or a game of passion.

The game is played by two players who, via the use of cards or certain plays, come to the conclusion of the game with the recommendation of various sexual positions to explore. There are almost 30,000 possible combinations, allowing you to try something different every time.

Heart of Erotica

Erotic Heart, another game for couples that are offered under multiple titles depending on the importer, is likewise built on similar concepts. However, its name comes from the fact that it is given in a heart-shaped container directly out of the box.

There are multiple wrapped-up notes within that the couples may fish one at a time. Each one indicates a punishment, but a very lovely penance since it has an erotic aspect that the partner or companion would undoubtedly like.

The bonding that is gentle

There are other simpler games to play that do not need spending money or going to a store. Bondage, for example, has been used for a very long time using very basic materials like ribbons or handkerchiefs (or even handcuffs and ropes if you want to go large).

Well, the game may be enjoyable, particularly if played in an undemanding manner. Soft bondage, in reality, does not include harmful bindings, but rather a few tiny games with laces and ribbons, preferably silk, in order to imagine and imitate even a little.

Food Smeared

Have you watched the last 9 1/2 weeks? In that film, the moment in which Mickey Rourke slides an ice cube over Kim Basinger's body is well-known.

It's a really sensual image, which many people sought to recreate at the time, even in their own closet.

Actually, you don't have to use ice. Indeed, the experience may be enhanced by the addition of additional items, particularly food. Consider whipped cream or strawberries, both of which are aphrodisiacs. In short, even here, imagination reigns supreme.

Apps for erotic pleasure

If your imagination isn't helping you come up with fresh sex games, you may use several sexy applications to put on your smartphone. Planet Pron, for example, has a large collection of films and free photographs to pique your interest, and for couples' sex games, you may pick between Ultimate Sex Games for Couples for iPhone and The Foreplay Game for Android. There is a Tantric Sex Deck if you wish to attempt tantric sex instead. The main thing to remember is that the applications are useful for experimenting. The phone must not become a bothersome third party! Unless you decide to use it for sexting: even if a couple is forced to remain apart, they may still have a hot moment. Indeed, at a distance, you may exchange sensual photographs, perhaps using an app that does not leave a trace, such as Snapchat, and texts with high erotic content. The sole precaution is to constantly be mindful of privacy and to engage in sexting only with people you trust, in order to prevent unpleasant inconveniences such as the dissemination of images and screenshots of discussions.

CHAPTER 6

PLAYING WITH SEX QUESTIONS ROMANTIC REVELATIONS

Softly caress your partner and urge them to share their amorous aspirations while you're in a calm condition before or after making love.

Communicate the joys that each of you wants to have.

Investigate each other's unique desires to make living that much more joyful. Discover each other's fancies and brainstorm methods to make them a reality.

Everyone has hidden sexual fantasies that they feel are too delicate, surprising, or strange to share even with their spouse. How can I help you feel more at ease discussing our hidden wants so that we may both fulfill them?

Some individuals feel that sexual fantasies should be kept private, while others believe that revealing them and even making them a reality may be enjoyable. What are your thoughts on us exploring and expressing our sexual fantasies?

What is your favorite feature of our lovemaking? Which of our sensual memories is your favorite?

How important do you think foreplay is for great sex? What factors contribute to successful foreplay?

If you had the opportunity to "see" all of a single person's sexual thoughts, ideas, and fantasies, whose mind would you want to read?

What is the "weirdest" dream you like and confess to having, but would never or could not perform in real life?

Do you feel kinky or sexually adventurous:

You are?

Who am I?

Could we be?

How interested in sex were you as a child? What did you do to quench your need for knowledge?

Excellent Foreplay

Use your imagination to immerse your beloved in a sexual encounter that will excite both their body and mind. Give your guests a feast for all five senses. Allow time to enjoy a variety of sensory pleasures. When you're ready to make love, try to make foreplay completely fantastic.

What do you think we can do to make foreplay more enjoyable? How would you want to spice up our pre-game?

How do you feel about trying out new creative foreplay techniques? What new forms of foreplay would you want to try?

How do you feel about being blinded while I delight you? What kinds of foreplay have you experienced while blindfolded?

What are your thoughts on viewing porn together as pre-play?

Assume we're building a penis mold that takes a long time to set. How long do you think "we" could keep an erection going, and what kinds of stimulation do you think would be necessary to keep it hard?

Do you prefer that our foreplay be spontaneous or planned? How do you prefer to change up your foreplay moves?

What is your favorite foreplay method that you

utilize to please me with?

Did I use to please you?

In a modern-day fantasy or role-playing situation, would you prefer to be: .

Doctor or a patient?

Client or escort?

Executive or administrative assistant?

Police officer or criminal

Photographer or fashion model?

Kissing Relationship

A person's kissing style is a good predictor of how they make love. Increase your kissing style and breadth of methods, and your expertise as a sensuous lover will certainly improve. Kissing should never be taken for granted, even in long-term partnerships. Learn how to kiss correctly and practice often. Combine various kisses in sexual patterns of exquisite bliss. Kissing is a great way to connect with your sweetheart.

How significant do you think kissing is? How can one become a better kisser?

How do you think we can enhance the way we kiss each other? What can I do to enhance the way I kiss you?

Other than on the lips, where do you like to be kissed?

Which lipstick color do you think is the most kissable?

Which lipstick color do you think is the sexiest for oral sex?

Would you prefer to retake or relive your first passionate kiss? How do you think we might recapture the ecstasy of our initial make-out sessions?

Have you ever had or given someone the following:

An electric kiss?

What about an upside-down kiss?

Is it a vampire kiss or a hickey?

How about a snowball kiss?

When and where did you first learn to kiss? What more do you think we should know about kissing?

What constitutes a good kiss? What kind of kissing do you prefer?

Exploration of Erogenous Zones

Explore your lover's whole body with your lips and tongue. Resist the desire to focus on what you already know. Create a map of new territory. Add some warm and cold breaths to help stimulate any sensitive regions you find.

Which of my erogenous zones do you believe is the most sensitive? Which portion of my body do you like stimulating the most?

Which of your erogenous zones or portions of your body would you want me to massage during foreplay?

More touching and caressing?

More kissing and licking?

Continue to rub and massage?

What should you avoid?

How would you feel about french kissing with someone of the same sex?

Are you doing a handjob?

Getting a handjob?

Having oral sex?

Do you have sex together?

Can you think of any more sorts of nipple stimulation? What kind of nipple stimulation do you prefer?

What home objects do you think you and your partner might utilize to make each other happy? What were we going to do with them?

What is the most creative foreplay method you've ever seen or heard of?

How would you want to tease and tempt me throughout our sexual encounter?

How can we make our sex play more imaginative and erotically daring, in your opinion?

Luscious lips

Use your lips to stimulate your sweetheart in unexpected or long-desired ways. Investigate their physique for secret erogenous zones or have a sensual kiss. Keep your lips supple at all times.

What is your favorite advice or method for having fantastic oral sex with:

Is it a man?

Is it a woman?

If I were nude and pretended to be a statue standing completely motionless, what would you do with only your tongue to get me to move?

What are your thoughts on kissing after obtaining oral sex?

Which of the following colors do you connect with the word:

Love?

Sensual?

Sexy?

Intense?

Delectable?

Delectable?

Obnoxious?

Are you kinky?

How often do you want me to perform oral sex for you as **A.** foreplay? **B.** your climax?

What are your thoughts on gender reversal and gender play?

What types of situations do you think we could act out?

Is there a foreplay method you'd want to attempt that we haven't yet? What is one sexual action you'd want to attempt that neither of us has done before?

What types of items do you think we'd purchase online if we were both condemned to house imprisonment for 6 months with no other responsibilities?

A Caring Touch

Use your fingers as delicate pleasure instruments. Touch and brush your lover's whole body with affection. Sensitize their skin as you gradually search for new erogenous zones. Allow yourself plenty of time to tease and tantalize them until their genitals throb with want.

How does having sex vary from making love, in your opinion?

What is your finest foreplay advise if you were giving it to: a.

a woman?

Is he a man?

Are you a lesbian?

Is he a homosexual man?

Are there any foreplay behaviors or practices that you believe ought to be changed?

Do you have any sex toys that you'd want me to utilize with you during our sex play?

Have you ever played in a threesome or a moresome? If we were to invite another individual or couple to join us, who would you invite and how would you see us accomplishing it?

.What would we have done together if we had won a trophy for the most wonderful sex scene?

.Think of a happy-ending love tale that we've both recently viewed together. If you had to "end" the film with a sex scene, where would it take place and what would the actors be doing?

The Library of Love

When you hone your talents, making love may become an art form.

Becoming a master of intimacy needs a great deal of practice, as well as knowledge and a willingness to study. Invest in a private love library. Learn ways for being creative that go beyond your imagination. Find inspiration for new fantasies. As you find the thrill of studying, your confidence will grow. Purchase a new love book for your collection now.

What activities do you engage in to broaden your sex knowledge?

What is your favorite sort of erotica to read?

50. In a fantasy or role-playing situation set in ancient times, which of the following would you choose to be:

a. Priest or worshiper?

b. The knight or the rescued?

c. Missionary or barbarian?

d. Inquisitor or witch?

e. Traveler or local?

If we were to collaborate on an erotic fiction, what would it be about?

What kind of sex education did you get, and how are you continuing to educate yourself?

53. What types of items would you have placed in a sexual scrapbook or memory box if you had begun one as a teenager?

When it comes to fun things we can do together, I'm curious:

a. Where do you obtain your sex play ideas?

b. Where do you go to get innovative ideas?

c. How can we generate fresh concepts to test?

What major incidents in your love life would you want to document if you could travel back in time and capture photographs or movies of your sexual history?

Are there any foreplay skills that you believe we should acquire or relearn?

CHAPTER 7

CHALLENGE SEX GAMES

What Exactly Is A Sex Challenge Game?

It's when you're attempting to do a task while having sex. It's frequently an activity that requires some work and attention, making it difficult to perform both the task and a pleasant sex session.

But it doesn't mean we can't have some fun while we're doing it.

After all, it is only through trials and pushing ourselves to our limitations that we discover our true capabilities and interests.

Above all, it's simply exciting to attempt to make sex into a game that you can win. As we all know, it's easy to get hooked to games that we haven't yet mastered, thus these sex games may also urge you to have sex more regularly.

These don't have to be done or applied during foreplay or intercourse; they may be done and applied anytime you want to spice things up.

The Lava Monster

Remember when you were a kid and you used to play on the swings and you had to keep off the gravel or tanbark? It included swinging from bar to bar and jumping from one area to the concrete and back.

Consider this in the context of sex. The floor (carpet, rug, wood, whatever you want to call it) has suddenly changed into blazing hot lava, and you are not allowed to touch it! You may have sex everywhere except on the floor, but your mission is to advance from one room to the next.

You can only take three steps on the floor at a time before you need to leap upon a table, counter, or chair and resume having sex. You also only get three steps in between sex.

The more inventive you are, the more enjoyable this will be. Begin in the kitchen and make your way to your bed, aided only by a couple of chairs and a rug. How about attempting to figure out postures that would work when one of you is standing and the other is awkwardly twisted, trying to keep balanced? Or how about wandering around the home, taking off your clothes, and then having to follow that trail of clothing back to the bedroom without touching the floor underneath?

Remember that you may utilize items other than furniture. In a pinch, you may even take a nearby magazine or blanket and put it on the floor to use. Have fun and be resourceful. It's best to begin by traveling from one area to the next, with lots of stuff in between.

When you're ready for a tougher challenge, you may go across the home and return, utilizing items that only enable one person to stay stable at a time.

A Single Finger

Some may find this difficult, while others may find it incredibly simple! The goal is to make your spouse orgasm with just one finger. You take turns and the one who completes this task the quickest wins. Other props, such as pornography, may be used, but physical contact must be restricted to one finger.

Men can finger, massage, and penetrate. You would believe that the guy has an edge here since it's simpler to concentrate on a clitoris with one finger than a penis.

That may be true, yet there are several methods for women to stimulate a penis with only one finger. Simply concentrate on the top of the penis, or wrap it around for a one-finger handjob if your fingers are long enough. If it remains imbalanced, just shift the goalposts such that success for a guy implies two orgasms while a win for a woman means only one orgasm.

This will require you to be inventive and resourceful once again, asking yourself, "How can I make an orgasm happen within these constraints?"

After all, necessity is the mother of innovation, and you may be devising some unconventional methods to achieve mutual pleasure.

Pursue That Feeling

This sex game is about remembering and reliving earlier emotional and physical highs.

Each partner will recall the finest sex they've ever had as a pair — with that particular partner. Then you will reflect on all of the factors that led up to it - what, where, when, why, and how. Try to remember as much as you can about it, even if you have to fill in the blanks with assumptions.

It's acceptable if your and your partner's finest sex moments don't coincide. That just means you'll take turns.

After you've filled in all the specifics about that time, you'll attempt to recreate that sexual experience as nearly as possible using what you've noted.

If it occurred on the beach and you're not near it, apply sunscreen, listen to ocean noises, and sit on a blanket on the ground. If it was in your vehicle, take it to a dark alley (or maybe simply your backyard) and execute the act there, while listening to the same music and wearing the same clothing. If it happened in your bed after a long date, go to the same restaurant and order the same dishes before coming home to do the dirty.

Simply attempt to match the settings as closely as possible. This makes this game a great planning event for you two as well since it requires you to collaborate to design the setting.

As for real intercourse, try to imitate it as well! Who made the initial move, what transpired, what positions you were in, and how the first attempt at penetration was made. If you recall, you might attempt to imitate the positions you employed as well as how and where you orgasmed. Did they do anything that piqued your interest or astonished you? Did you snuggle and prepare for round two, or did you have to hide from your partner's parents?

You're pursuing an old memory while also developing a new one and maybe improving on it.

Give It a Name

This sex game will put your instincts to the test. You'll both be nude. One person will be blindfolded, while the other will control the game. The partner in control will entertain the blinded partner with an item for up to sixty seconds, and the recipient will have three chances to determine what the object is.

If the recipient gets it right the first three times, they get anything they want for the next sixty seconds. If they are incorrect, they must switch roles and blindfold the other partner. It will be more enjoyable if you utilize your imagination rather than sex devices.

You may substitute household items, food, clothes, unusual portions of your body, or even sports equipment. What you can use to please your lover is simply limited by your imagination.

Maintain Rhythm

Music during sex is nearly always a positive to establish the tone and create the illusion that you are in your own world.

This game takes things a step further by compelling you to have sex to the rhythm of the music playing. To accomplish this most efficiently, choose a YouTube playlist that alternates between tracks or rhythms every sixty seconds. If it's simpler for you, you may also set your standard music playlist to shuffle. Just make sure the songs that play after each other are random and vary in pace and rhythm.

Begin listening to this music as you begin foreplay, but you should really start paying attention when you begin intercourse. Keep the beat, keep in sync, and adjust as the song changes every minute. This will provide you with a lot of variation to experiment with, as well as ensuring that the male and female spend equal time on top since the partner on top is basically who controls the rhythm.

It would probably be worth your effort to create a playlist of 60-second clips ahead of time, merely to guarantee that the songs have a variety of rhythms and speeds. Songs from salsa, electronica, tango, and country, for example, are all quite diverse and will make you move in very different ways. At the very least, you may find new songs you like.

Contest of Stars

This is certainly a game you played as a kid or with your pet, but it takes on a whole new meaning in this context.

This is primarily intended for usage during intercourse. You and your partner will only have sex in this game if you can maintain eye contact. Whatever you want to swivel into missionary, cowgirl, side. Make every effort to keep eye contact throughout, and don't break it until absolutely necessary.

A point is deducted from the partner who is the first to look away or break eye contact.

This game is played on a point system, with the partner with the highest score (who breaks eye contact the least) getting to pick a prize.

The gazing contest sex game is fantastic for a variety of reasons.

For starters, it strengthens your bond as a pair. That's what persistent eye contact can accomplish, and it may give you the impression that you can sense their spirit as well as their body. Because of this, you may find that this session is more intense than usual.

Second, the closer we get to climax, the more we feel the desire to look away or shut our eyes. That provides a nice twist and puts you both on an equal footing!

Groping in Public

We're all a little bit of an exhibitionist.

This game involves attempting to sexually contact your spouse as many times as possible in public.

The following is the scoring system:

1 point for grope penis/vagina over clothing

2 points for grope penis/vagina beneath clothing.

3 points for groping the penis/vagina over the garments for 5 seconds.

4 points for groping the penis/vagina beneath garments for 5 seconds.

Oral underwear (must last at least 3 seconds): 6 points

You can see what you should prioritize if you want to get the most points! If you are caught, which means that a member of the public notices what you are doing, you will not get the points. If the above is too brave or too tame for you, feel free to add further levels.

Set the time limit for this game to be a whole day, a trip to the mall, an errand, or a meal out. Just make sure you agree on it ahead of time so you don't wind up kissing your partner in front of their parents.

Even if you're competing, you may both wear attire that makes this easy for both of you. Skirts without underwear, elastic waistlines, short shorts, giant baggy shirts, massive handbags, gigantic caps, and so forth. If it still seems too unsafe, you may make it simpler by cutting holes at the crotch, in pockets, or in trousers so your lover can grope you in private.

It will also assist to consider particular spots where you may do this, such as picture booths, automobiles, dark corners, public toilets, behind buildings, and dressing rooms.

Public groping may begin as harmless fun, but can quickly escalate into super-hot sexual tension, pushing you to rush home from the gym because you are very aroused. Errands have never looked better

CHAPTER 8

GAMES WITH SEX TOYS

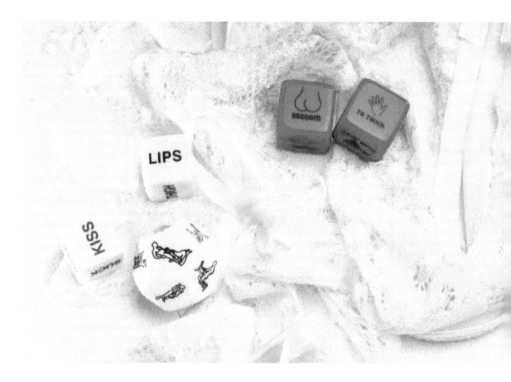

Scrabble is hot and dirty.
You'll Need:

Get a Scrabble game and place it in a comfortable area with a few sex toys of your choosing.

You should both start to scrabble with your clothes on. Make a list of and agree on the winner's sexual favor or award.

Playing Instructions

The purpose of Hot and Dirty Scrabble is to create words that reflect desire, passion, and love for your significant other. Try to come up with phrases that will stimulate them and make them hot for lovemaking. Get each other naked and conduct foreplay activities according to the terms you made. The person who comes up with the highest score for a term is the winner and will earn the prize you established beforehand. Play conventional scrabble as usual, but with the following extra rules:

• Slang phrases are acceptable in this edition as long as they are connected to sex.

• If the words are seductive and triggering, multi-word combinations (without gaps) may be employed (e.g., glass dildo, butt plug lick my)

• Only one article of clothes may be removed every round for stripping.

• Double or triple time will be awarded for putting sexual words on bonus squares. Here are some words that may be used to elicit arousal.

• Shirt: I'll carefully unbutton your shirt.

• Flavor: As I lick and suck your breast, let me enjoy the flavor of this strawberry syrup.

• Glass: Enjoy a glass of dildo as I keep an eye on you.

• Black: Satisfy allows me to please you with this black vibrator if you open your legs.

• Paint: Apply lube to the clitoris and nipples using a clean brush.

The Extender

What You'll Need: An extender is utilized on the male partner for this game. It's a shaft designed to fit over his penis to provide length and maybe girth. This may be done at home or even at a hotel.

Playing Instructions:

When the male partner employs this, he may be seen as a new or distinct person by the female partner. Perhaps the two partners could play out the female character's affair. When the extension is employed, this may even result in a stay in a hotel room. Exploring even the most common sexual acts or positions with this extender may be pleasant, since the feelings may be entirely novel to both parties.

Allow the female player to do a "hand job" or oral sex on the guy. The male partner may get fresh pleasure from witnessing his large new companion enter the female spouse.

Game of Remote Control Orgasm

What you'll need: Are you planning a road trip soon? Bring along a new toy: a remote control vibrator. Include some spare batteries as well.

Playing Instructions:

You surprise her with a nicely wrapped present before you depart for your vacation. She laughs, stuffs it into a bag, and walks away. You make her put it on. The goal of this game is to make her aroused, then calm her down—until she is demanding you to stop the vehicle and do her right now! Tease her with it, arouse her, then turn it off. Give her an orgasm (or numerous) with cunnilingus when you get at your destination (or stop off the road into a rest area).

• Begin by synchronizing vibrating speed with traffic signals.

Give her a mild buzz as you get to a red light. Accelerate when the light turns green.

• Alternatively, sync the buzz with music.

• When you arrive at a secluded rest stop, show gallantry by opening her door, assisting her, and putting her on her back, feet up, on the front hood like a hood ornament. There aren't any privacy options? Place her in the rear seat of the car.

• Hold the vibration on her clit for a few seconds as you play in her vagina.

• Now, turn off the vibration. Using a flat tongue, run it up and down the inside of her inner lips.

• Pay close attention to her clitoris. Tap the sides of your tongue with the tip of your tongue. Swish it about with your tongue. Tap the clitoris's tip.

• Suck on her and twirl her around for orgasm.

Vibrator Salesman Who Goes Door-to-Door
What you'll require:

A suit, briefcase, brochures, and, most importantly, a variety of vibrators are required.

Playing Instructions:

Simply put on a suit and pose as a door-to-door vibrator salesperson. Try to catch your partner off guard while she thinks you're at work or doing something else.

Ring the doorbell, then enter the home and inform her that you have some extremely interesting things to show her. Take the vibrators out one at a time, taking your time with each one and explaining which are best suited for specific forms of play. Ask her if she'd like to borrow one and test it out (while you keep an eye on her, of course)! You may also try the one below for diversity.

Come inside the home and establish the ground rules: You can only show her the items if she is nude, therefore the first thing she must do is strip-down (or change into something comfy, such as a short and seductive bathrobe). Furthermore, whether she likes it or not, you will show their efficacy on her. You may now take out some silk ties or handcuffs and bind her arms or legs to a chair leg. Then go through the product line one by one, spending as much time as you need to show how successful the gadgets are for stimulation, teasing, and maybe even orgasm. Are you ready to take things to the next level? Request that she switches roles and test the vibrators on you — maybe you'd want to try anal stimulation!

Excellent Vibrations

What you'll require:

Set a sensual tone for your night of pleasure by doing the following: Make a fire, dim the lights, and play some sensual music. Prepare a blindfold and line up all of your vibrating gadgets, whether it's the cone, a little clit vibrator, or whatever in between.

Remember, the goal of this game is to tease every inch of your lover's body with a variety of vibrators! Slowly undress your beloved, kiss her passionately, and run your hands over her body, telling her how hot and seductive she is. Lead her to the vibrating pleasure zone while blindfolding her. Begin gently, possibly with a vibrating wand on her neck and shoulders. Use a different vibrating gadget on different places of your body: Massage her muscles with long, flowing strokes, then tease her nipples with a vibrating finger gadget before moving on to her genitals. You may use a vibrator to tease open her labia, then switch gears to reach her G-spot before returning to her clitoris for the ultimate climax!

Use a set of vibrating nipple clips to keep her on her toes while inserting a vibrating butt plug or having her grind on a cone-like gadget. Turn on the U-shaped vibrator after she's hot and wet and stimulate her G-spot and clitoris at the same time. Allow her to ride the vibrations all the way to heaven and back! Begin with her toes and two or three of your favorite vibrating gadgets. Moving gently, try each gadget on every inch of her, being sure to test every speed, pulsation, and pattern. Maintain the tension by avoiding the genitals until her clitoris is completely engorged, and keep her wondering where you're heading next and what it'll feel like.

Party of Pleasure

What you'll require: The Sexy Setup Invite your partner to a "pleasure party" for two. Tell him you have a unique collection of tools and tricks that will keep him entertained for hours. Set a romantic and sensual scene: Make a nest of blankets and furs on the floor, light some candles, and put on your most seductive lingerie. Line up all of your sex toys, but conceal them with a silky scarf.

Playing Instructions:

Begin by kissing your sweetheart long and lingeringly, then undress him half and ask him to get comfortable. Tell him you're the mistress of pleasure and that you're going to show him all of your instruments. Bring out your sex toys one at a time and use them on different regions of his body, increasing the tension and excitement as you go. Massage his neck and shoulders with a vibrator, then softly buzz his nipples with a vibrating finger gadget. As you touch his penis, move your gadget down his body and tickle his perineum or around his testicles.

Use each item to turn him on for a few moments, but don't let him go all orgasmic—stop and introduce the next toy until he's ready to explode!

Then assist him in climaxing in whichever manner seems most natural to him!

To heat things even further, assist your sweetheart in totally undressing and inviting him into the pleasure nest. Show him all you have, but then blindfold him and bind his wrists over his head. As you apply the toy to his body, tell him he must guess what it is. If he guesses right, you'll give him a kiss (or a sip of champagne, a morsel of chocolate, etc.), but if he guesses poorly, he may receive a spanking or a mild smack. Try out your toys one at a time and think creatively: Use your vibrating gadgets on various parts of his body, then put on a cock ring and ride him for a few minutes before jumping off and inserting his penis into a sleeve. Keep him guessing till he can't anymore! If you're feeling brave, try out several toys at once: Insert a strand of anal beads, and then suck him off while pressing your bullet vibrator at the base of his penis. Pull out the beads exactly as he reaches his peak!

The Hole of Glory

What you'll need: a suction cup dildo, a glory hole is described as a tiny hole in a wall where the guy can fit his penis through and the person on the other side may caress it. It would be ideal to get a dildo with a suction cup backing that would enable it to attach to a wall for this experiment.

Playing Instructions:

This may simulate the image of another guy staying nameless behind the wall, allowing the two lovers to act-out distinct fantasies with the "third person."

Both couples might take turns "heading" the fictitious individual. While doing oral sex with the male partner, the female partner might use the dildo to enter herself. In essence, she would be in command of her penetration. If the male partner so desired, he could even use it for anal penetration. If a higher degree of risk is wanted, the dildo might be transported to locations where a glory hole could be located, such as gas stations, public toilets, or adult theaters.

CHAPTER 9

ADVANCED SEX GAMES FOR DARING COUPLES

Perhaps you and your spouse have previously dabbled in sex games and want to take things to the next level, or you just want to try out some more daring activities. So don't worry, we've got you covered. According to a study, couples that regularly participate in novel activities such as sex games have greater levels of pleasure than couples who do not. Couples might have a more fascinating existence together by playing sex games.

The games we will discuss will be a combination of fully free possibilities that will simply demand your creativity, as well as some that will require you to purchase anything. As usual, get your partner's permission before attempting anything new in bed.

Sexy Shopping Therapy

This one will need you and your companion to go shopping. This may be done in person or online. You may both choose things you want to see the other wear, or one of you can choose clothing for the other, whatever works best for you.

Have some fun seeing their jaws drop as you get dressed after the clothes come.

Dare and Drive

We've previously spoken about how a lot of individuals think the concept of doing anything kinky outdoors or in public is exciting. So you can get crazy outside with this game. To play this game, both of you must dress in scant attire. It might be a seductive black gown or thin shorts and a basic t-shirt. Then go for a short drive. You will each propose a location where you will halt. When you come to a halt, the person who picked the location will be challenged by his or her companion to walk out and do something bad.

Keep the daring low-key to avoid drawing too much attention to yourself. Then, as you begin your journey back home, begin to move your hand up your partner's leg to indicate that you want to do something together.

Rip It Apart

Have you ever wanted to have wild, rip-your-clothes sex but didn't want to ruin your clothes? Then you should give this game a go. All you need to do is go out and get some inexpensive clothing. A thrift shop might be an excellent choice. Wash them, dress them, and then inform your spouse that they are free to tear them to pieces.

There are plenty of additional methods to destroy it. You may either let your carnal passion go and enjoy a rip-fest, or you can integrate ripping into a points-based game. It is all up to you. If you like having rough sex, you will enjoy this.

Pong with Stripes

This elevates beer pong to an all-new level. Clear your dining table, then arrange six plastic cups in the shape of a triangle. Fill the cups with beer or your favorite alcoholic beverage, and then take turns attempting to hurl a ping pong ball into the cups of the other person. When a player scores, their partner must take what is in the cup where the ball landed and then remove a piece of clothing. The first individual to get a ball into all six cups gets to request something special.

It's Toy Tease Time!

While retail therapy is all about appearances, this game allows you to test out the things you've always wanted. Again, you can go to a sex store in person or shop online, but get some sex toys you've always wanted to try. Don't be concerned if you don't know where to begin. To make this game more enjoyable, compile a list of things you've always wanted to try and offer it to your partner. They may then purchase whatever items are on that list that they want. You can play a quick game once the items arrive. You will be blindfolded and on the bed, and your companion will gently tease you with the toys one at a time. They will bring you to orgasm with it if you can guess what it is in three guesses.

Position Difficulties

This is the perfect game to play if you want a game that will also help your sex linger longer. The fundamental goal of the game is simple: see how many various positions you and your partner can accomplish in one sex session until you both experience orgasm. The longer you play this game, the better it becomes since you may strive to outdo yourself.

Heaven in Seven Minutes

Have you ever gotten to savor the thrill of squeezing in a quickie before someone walks in and finds out? This is the game that will allow you to relive the exhilaration of having a limited amount of time to complete a task. Set a timer for seven minutes for you and your companion. Then locate a private spot, such as a closet, and see if the two of you can knock off a quickie before your time runs out.

This may be an exciting and enjoyable game that brings the two of you closer together.

Housewarming

The purpose of the party is to keep an orgasm at bay. Nobody can climax until you've banged in every room of your home. All you have to do is attempt to have sex in each room before climaxing. This game may also be used as a sort of foreplay.

The Master of Oral Communication

If your foreplay game seems to be missing, try the oral master game. Set a timer for four minutes and see who can start the most oral sex positions before the timer runs out. Make sure to keep track, and then you may switch roles to see who is the master of oral sex. This also allows you to learn a few other oral sex positions, which is particularly useful if your previous expertise was restricted to a kneeling blow job.

The Orgasm Race

This game is all about mutual masturbation and is the perfect game to play to bring you and your partner closer together. Because most individuals masturbate alone, doing so in front of others will heighten your sensation of vulnerability and aid to strengthen your closeness. This will also enable you to demonstrate to your lover precisely what you want and how you want it.

You will like next to each other and begin pleasuring one other to have an orgasm race. Whoever climaxes first wins and will continue to delight their companion until they climax. You may even stipulate that the slim winner receives a sexy little reward the next time you do it.

Identify the Letter

This is another game that may be used to spice up your oral sex and foreplay.

This game is a fun approach to getting to know your partner's physique. All you have to do is lay them down, blindfold them, and then choose your favorite regions of their body, such as their genitals, breasts, or belly. Then you'll delicately shape a letter onto their skin, keeping the motions tantalizing and light. They get one point if they correctly guess the letter. When they obtain ten right answers, they achieve an orgasm, and you switch places.

Insert It Into My Mouth

Nothing surpasses the combination of sex and food for increasing your desire levels. To play this game, you must strip nude, blindfold your partner, and then they will serve you various delectable dishes. You may choose any of your favorite meals, but sweet foods, such as strawberries, yogurt, ice cream, cake, or the traditional, chocolate, are often the greatest when accompanied with sex.

Because your companion is blindfolded, the spoon will end up in a variety of locations. And there is one basic rule: whatever is spilled on you must be licked off. You may direct them to the appropriate locations. This is an excellent game for developing trust, and you will enjoy the feeling of having food licked off of your body.

CHAPTER 10

SEX GAMES WITH DRINKS

Tango Requires Two

When it comes to alcoholic beverages and sex games, one can't help but think of the many traditional hot sex games that may be done. To begin, all that is required is an empty bottle, which may be any kind of alcohol.

Simply flip the bottle around and act out the one that was requested.

Different sorts of kisses must be offered to you when the bottle points to your companion. Also, if you want to add some taste to the game, you may use whipped cream or chocolate spread, depending on your preference, and if the end of the bottle points to your partner, he must lick it off your body and relish in whatever food you choose to heighten the sexual tension.

Heads or Butts or Sexy Coin Toss

The original coin toss game has been converted into a passionate, seductive, and filthy version that couples will enjoy. Each time the coin is flipped, each of you must gamble the opposite way, predicting whether it will land on heads or tails. The person who does not consider it properly shall drink one shot and remove one item of clothes. The games will conclude when one of you is completely nude, paving the way for more passionate and seductive foreplay.

Shots of Boozy Body

One of the most basic and easy erotic booze games, all you need are two dice, a notepad and paper, shot glasses, and your favorite alcoholic beverage. Write the various sections of the body on the portion of the paper, fold it, and assign a number to each piece of paper. The player will next roll the dice and get the matching numbered piece of paper. The shot of liquor must be taken from whichever bodily area is specified.

The Game Is to Keep a Straight Face

Give each of you and your spouse a sheet of paper on which you will list 6-12 wicked, nasty, and sexy terms without disclosing them to one another.

When finished, fold each cut piece of paper and place it into a dish. With each round, you and your partner will pick one piece of paper and attempt to repeat it loudly enough for everyone to hear without displaying any emotion. If you and your partner can maintain a straight face, no consequences will be imposed. One of you who will exhibit a hint of emotion, such as a smile, laugh, or grimace, must take one shot.

Twister with Hot Vodka

Twister's fundamental principle is balance, and adding the aspect of becoming intoxicated will make it more interesting and a lot more enjoyable. Play the game as normal, but for a twist, place many vodka shots and various glasses of water on the sheet's number.

Drink the shot on the number after spinning it before placing your leg or hand on it. You're in luck if you drink a shot of water. All of this drinking, caressing, and getting near to one other's bodies will ultimately lead to a night in the bedroom.

Game of Steamy Eye Contact (Don't Blink Or Else)

This is your moment to look each other in the eyes without feeling embarrassed. You must remain steady and avoid blinking your eyes while staring into each other's eyes. The person who blinks must take a shot and remove one article of clothing. This game will heighten the sense of sexual anticipation and tension between you two. Perhaps you can dress provocatively, making it harder for them to focus on staring into your eyes.

Treasure Map for the Body (X Marks the Spot)

If you've been seeking an opportunity and a cause to kiss your love, now is the time. The basic purpose of this game is to recall where you wish to be kissed and licked with your lips and tongue. Give your spouse four opportunities to determine where your favorite X location is. If they guessed correctly, you'll be kissed and licked on that place, but if they didn't, they'll have to drink three shots of your preferred booze. Continue to play, guess, and kiss until both of you are hot and intoxicated to finish it off in the bedroom.

Q&A about striptease

The first stage in this game is to think of one word, which might be a thing, a person, a location, an animal, or an emotion. Don't tell your partner the word just yet. Allow them three guesses at the term and allow them to ask you questions that you may respond with a yes or no to give them hints. They must offer a response to each question they ask, and if they get it wrong, your partner must take a shot and kiss you wherever you like. If they are unable to give the word, your partner must do lap dance and a striptease for you, and you know what happens next.

Erotic Touch Blinded

Blindfolds are often regarded as one of the most sexual items available for use in foreplay and seduction. This might be because when other senses are hindered, the remaining ones become more acute. All emotions will be amplified, and a simple touch will seem more intense while you are blinded. Having said that, if you want to spice up your next drinking session, this game is a must-play. The initial step is to blindfold one of you, then the other will function as the guide, placing the index finger on various places of the body (preferably the erogenous zones). The person wearing the blindfold must then guess which body part they are touching. If your partner fails to provide the right body part, he must take a shot; if he does, you must take a shot.

CHAPTER 11

BRILLIANT IDEAS FOR BLOWING YOUR PARTNER'S MIND IN BED

Investing time in mastering the principles of this book will help you give your spouse mind-blowing orgasms. Some individuals find it difficult to attain orgasm, but if you have the necessary abilities, you can do so fairly effortlessly. Many important factors must be present for someone to experience orgasm. For a woman to climax, she must feel completely comfortable in her circumstances. When it comes to this, men have it a little easier.

However, it may be challenging for them at times as well.

The suggestions and methods you'll use to guarantee your woman has a mind-blowing orgasm will be quite different from those you'll use to ensure your male counterpart has his. Different strategies will be used in various scenarios. It does not have to be tough to guarantee that your spouse experiences orgasm if you have the knowledge and capacity to do so. Let's look at both sexes and what you can do to guarantee that they enjoy mind-blowing orgasms every time you have a sexual interaction.

We'll begin by taking a look at the females. There are many things you may do to make it easier for her to have an orgasm. Most women confess to having staged a few orgasms throughout their lives. Unfortunately, a handful is a significant underestimation of how many times most women have cheated. It's awful that they think they have to do this to make their sexual partners happy. Men, keep in mind that you cannot force a woman to have an orgasm. It will take time, and there will be moments when she will just be unable to get there. This is OK since the sense of sexual connection is satisfying enough when orgasm is not possible.

The atmosphere in which you place your woman will have a large impact on whether or not she can climax. As previously said, ladies must be at ease and calm to have an orgasm.

So, if you want to guarantee that your wife has an orgasm every time you engage in sexual intercourse, establishing the tone for her is more vital than ever.

We cannot emphasize enough how crucial it is to take your time and spend it in 4 plays. This strategy will assist to warm her up before the real intercourse occurs. A girl needs time to get genuinely aroused, and foreplay will certain that she is. You may excite all of her erogenous zones with your tongue or your hands and have her reeling when it's time to enter her.

You should bear in mind that most women reach climax in around 20 minutes on average. When a guy ejaculates before this, it may be quite inconvenient for the woman.

Don't leave her stranded if you can't last any longer to give her the time she needs to climax. You may please her after you've attained climax to guarantee she receives hers as well. It may be a little messy, but she will surely love it if you opt to finish her off with a couple of fingers after you have climaxed.

Another excellent suggestion for ensuring that your wife achieves climax is to concentrate on her clitoris. Most women are unable to attain orgasm with mere penetration. From the female's point of view, the combination of penetration with clitoral stimulation is incredible. Most women would prefer that you only concentrate on their clitoris to assist them in reaching climax. Penetration is amazing, and most women like it; but, it is unlikely to be enough to genuinely bring her there.

You should also make an effort to promote nasty discussion. Being a jerk before and during intercourse may be quite exciting. It turns on ladies and enables them to unwind. Most women do not want to engage in a sexual experience with a bashful guy. So, be courageous and open your voice to express all of your aspirations and ambitions. It will be much appreciated by her.

Last but not least, try to locate her G-spot. Yes, the G-spot does exist. It is usually found a few inches within her vagina on the front wall. You may trigger her G-spot with a little pressure and a circular pattern of movement. This may result in female ejaculation and some of the finest orgasms she has ever had. If you add some clitoral stimulation to the mix, you'll be driving her insane.

Let's flip the roles now that we've looked at a few things that guys may do to guarantee that their women have fantastic orgasms.

Some folks may find it difficult to figure out just what to do to guarantee that he gets a mind-blowing orgasm. This is particularly true if you lack experience. Remember that sex is a learning process, and the more you do it, the better you will get. Furthermore, the better your communication with your spouse, the simpler it will be to perform the things that please them.

While it may be simpler to give your partner an orgasm than for him to give you one, you should be aware that there are various degrees. Some male orgasms are just OK, while others are truly out of this world. We want to give our male counterparts orgasms that are constantly out of this world. Let's have a look at some various approaches that may assist you in doing this.

Men, like women, must be calm and undistracted to experience orgasm. Setting the tone may help them throw their everyday concerns out of their heads and concentrate on the closeness that is about to begin. Furthermore, foreplay is nearly as crucial for males as it is for women. This escalation. It increases sexual tension and makes intercourse much more exciting.

When intimacy is done well, both parties are completely focused on one other. This often results in a guy postponing his orgasm until his female counterpart is fulfilled. Telling your boyfriend he doesn't have to worry about you is one method to assure he has a mind-blowing climax. Make the sexual encounter solely about him. Allow him to relax while you take command. Encourage him to climax whenever possible, even if it is a brief climax. This may be immensely liberating for a partner and lower their level of concern, allowing them to experience a mind-blowing orgasm.

Withholding it for a few days is another wonderful piece of advice that might assist your boyfriend to have a mind-blowing orgasm. Yes, this may be challenging for both sides. This is particularly true if you have a real sexual relationship. You may spice up both sides to have very strong orgasms by withholding actual intercourse. It will take some effort, but you will both be grateful in the end.

Another thing you can do to assist your boyfriend to have a mind-blowing orgasm is to surprise him. Most women do not start a quickie in the afternoon. It is, however, something that should be done more regularly. Surprising him with a spontaneous tumble in the covers may significantly increase his degree of enjoyment and experience during intercourse.

The recommendations we've provided you to assist increase the number of orgasms for your spouse are just a few of the numerous things that work. If you've tried everything else, do some more research since there are other possibilities available. Simply attempting to guarantee that your spouse has good orgasms is a start in the right path, and the more you attempt, the more successful you will be.

CONCLUSION

Sex is wonderful because it is the consequence of passion and chemistry. Especially among couples, when love and creativity provide a lovely pleasurable moment in life. However, the light diminishes with time, and something must be done to keep it burning. Many couples are frequently troubled by worries about how to locate and rekindle that love after a long life together, including birthdays, debates, children, job and economic troubles, sickness, long-term home, everyday affairs, and law. This fire, this sexual need, defined the early years of their partnership.

Monotony may suffocate desire, and anybody who has lived in a sexless marriage knows this to be true. Sex and passion may be taken away from any circumstance that leads to routine, so even a lengthy relationship, even if it is not sealed by a married partnership, is not immune to this danger.

Monotonous everyday life, tension, exhaustion from a life that is not always easy, and daily challenges may lead a partner's personal life to fade into the background, with more or less serious consequences for stability. If all of these scenarios occur, or if, at some point during the marriage, the physiological decline of desire occurs and sex is a distant memory, and the couple is aware of what is happening and tries to maintain mentality, the couple will seriously consider how and with what strategy to maintain mentality.

Reacting is a manifestation of reproductive passion and desire.

Stress, despair, weariness, worry, involvement, and a lack of time may all be physical or psychological causes. First and foremost, you must consider if this is a regular occurrence or whether the unwillingness to take the initiative is new to the relationship. In contrast, if you discover that after you constantly want to make love, but the urge has fallen asleep from time to time, this might be a typical usage moment or a larger issue. A minor drop in a partner's libido over time is typical, but we don't have to be disheartened; sex may and can remain a crucial attachment for couples.

Desires may be readily maintained in healthy persons, even in the elderly. As a result, it is critical to comprehend the underlying causes of common issues and devise appropriate solutions. By napping throughout the routine, you may keep your sexiness clean.

1. Talk about your deterioration, even if it makes you uncomfortable. The fruit is seen by remembering this thorny thing, using the proper words, and without blaming anybody. You must be forthright and truthful. If there is a problem, if anything is wrong - even if it is sexual - speaking freely is the first and maybe most efficient method to remedy the issue. You must communicate to each other after you have done as little self-reflection as possible so that you can properly express to your spouse what issues need to be addressed. When you stop communicating with others, issues collect and go unaddressed, with predictable repercussions.

2. Shameless teasing Play, discover what inspires you the most, and turn passion into a pleasurable joy rather than a marital obligation.

3. Appease your partner's irritating dream. If a partner is constantly looking for something specific in sex and is never "satisfied," the moment of arousal may be the best time to attempt to fulfill them.

You are not required to do anything that you do not wish to do. If this is achievable, this choice of a path may open the door to a new dimension for personal life and couple life.

4. Schedule weekly sexual interactions. This may seem a touch sexual, but many studies believe it is the greatest option. That way, you can make it amusing, unique, and enjoyable.

5. Intimacy is more than simply having sex. Find links to your spouse without requesting an all-inclusive bundle. Massage, hugs, caresses, and kisses all contribute to closeness, however indirectly.

6. Think about the past. Look for the optimal time of action in your sex life and its qualities. Discuss it with them and let them know what you missed and what other portions of the apple desire.

7. The impact of surprise. It's normal to be rejected after a month if you eat spaghetti or pizza every day since you like them. Experiment with something new. If long-term relationship issues revolve around boredom and daily life, nothing beats doing new things and venturing into unexplored territory. It is sufficient to provide something new, but it is also necessary to surprise your spouse (maybe by dressing in your underwear more than normal) to adopt an attitude that the pair would not anticipate.

Outside of the house, sensuality. Plan exceptional gatherings, such as a stroll on the beach, a fireplace with background music, a highly romantic supper, and a steam bath. There may be sex without love, but there can't be love without sex.

8. Identify your moments. Even if you are recuperating from ordinary stress, it is a good idea to set aside at least one or two hours every week to commit yourself to your spouse, speak about aspirations and hopes, and depend on each other to discover closeness and compassion in times of danger. It is also beneficial to go out at any time or to take small breaks, such as a relaxing day or a romantic weekend. Affective closeness is also an essential aspect of good sexual partnerships. An excellent couple's vacation will be enough to fill the weekend. A weekend at a spa that blends passion regeneration with rest and well-being may be perfect.

9. Sex quality Reduced sexual activity is nearly "natural" as one becomes older and more involved, yet quality and quantity are sometimes misconstrued. In reality, frequency is not the most crucial component in having a fulfilling sex life. Better than frequent and rapid is unusual, but better than frequent and fast.

Daily use of sensitive and responsive behaviors in long-term couples may boost male and female sexual understanding and desire, particularly if this attitude offers a partner a feeling of worth. Understanding the needs of others, both emotionally and via listening, proximity, and love, boosts sexual desire, particularly when such sentiments convey the notion that the other person is worthwhile and that sexual interactions with a partner are very wanted.